DATE DUE

DISCARDED

Demco, Inc. 38-293

D1417776

GOLD MEDAL FOR WEIRD

KEVIN SYLVESTER

KIDS CAN PRESS

FEB 0 8 2008

Text and illustrations © 2007 Kevin Sylvester

Kids Can Press acknowledges the financial support of the Government of Ontario, through the Ontario Media Development Corporation's Ontario Book Initiative; the Ontario Arts Council; the Canada Council for the Arts; and the Government of Canada, through the BPIDP, for our publishing activity.

Published in Canada by
Kids Can Press Ltd.
29 Birch Avenue
Toronto, ON M4V 1E2

Published in the U.S. by
Kids Can Press Ltd.
2250 Military Road
Tonawanda, NY 14150

www.kidscanpress.com

Edited by Charis Wahl
Designed by Julia Naimska

Printed and bound in Singapore

CM PA 07 0 9 8 7 6 5 4 3 2 1

Library and Archives Canada Cataloguing in Publication

Sylvester, Kevin
Gold medal for weird / Kevin Sylvester.

ISBN 978-1-55453-021-2

1. Olympics—Anecdotes—Juvenile literature.
2. Olympics—Miscellanea—Juvenile literature. I. Title.
GV721.53.S94 2007   j796.48   C2007-901122-5

Kids Can Press is a CORUS™ Entertainment company

To all the athletes and sports figures who keep doing things worth celebrating — and laughing about.

Oh, yeah, and to my family, too!

GET YOUR BUTTS TO THE STARTING LINE!

Hey, welcome to our competition. We're just doing our stretches and warm-ups.

We've got a lot of events to cover, from swimming shark-infested waters to jumping over dead pigeons.

At most sporting events, athletes compete for the title of fastest, strongest, most artistic. Here, there are medals for goofiest, most dishonest and weirdest.

The big winter and summer Olympic events, held every two years, have given us amazing stories of achievement and success. If you want those, go get a different book. There are a few heroes in this one, but plenty of losers, cheaters and stuff that will just plain make you laugh 'til you puke.

So line up. The starting gun is about to go off.

BANG!

Here we go!

FIND THE MEDAL!
AND THE MEDALIST!

There are plenty of official records to tell you what happened at certain Olympics, but those results and statistics don't tell you the whole story. In fact, sometimes the whole story just — *poof!* — disappears.

Here are some of the stories that have fallen through the cracks.

Who was that young yeller-feller?

At the 1900 Paris Olympics, the Dutch rowing pairs team was one of the favorites; but they needed a coxswain to compete in their event. (The coxswain is the little person who sits at the end of a rowing boat, yelling, "ROW, ROW, ROW!" It gives the rowers a rhythm. So the cox has to be light and LOUD …)

The Dutch guys looked around the crowd, spotted a boy who didn't seem to weigh very much, and hauled him into the boat.

And boy, could that kid yell — the Dutch team won a very close race.

The boy posed for the victory photograph. Then he disappeared.

The rowers never found out his name or age, and, despite years of searching, he was never seen again.

Maybe the fish ate it?

The best boxer at the 1960 Rome Olympics was eighteen-year-old Cassius Clay (who later changed his name to Muhammad Ali). He won the gold medal and returned to his hometown of Louisville, Kentucky, expecting to be greeted as a hero.

But he wasn't. Clay was black, and this was the segregated U.S. south. According to his autobiography, Clay was refused service in a diner, even though he was wearing his gold medal. They didn't care that he'd won a medal for the U.S. They only saw his skin color. He says he got so sick of racism that he threw his gold medal into the river. Divers have searched for it from time to time but found nothing.

There is some debate about this story. Ali stood by it at first, but later said he might just have misplaced the medal.

However he lost it, Olympic officials gave him a replacement in a special ceremony in 1996.

8

Lucky loonie

The Canadian hockey teams were up against a lot of history at the 2002 Winter Games in Salt Lake City. The men hadn't won gold in decades. The women were on a big pre-Olympic losing streak. And the U.S. teams were on home ice and favored to win.

But in the finals, the Canadians seemed to have an extra bit of confidence — and luck. Bounces went their way, the other teams' shots hit the goalposts. People started to wonder if the Canadians were getting some outside help, especially when both the men and the women won their final games.

After the medal ceremonies, the ice-making crew 'fessed up. Yes, they'd helped out. The crew was from Canada and had buried a Canadian one-dollar coin under center ice.

Here's a funky fact … That coin now sits in the Hockey Hall of Fame. Canadian workers have hidden Canadian coins at other Olympic venues … like the dime under the speedskating ice in Turin.

Rhymes with poop...

Back in the 1990s, a group of Chinese runners stormed onto the world scene. They were all peasant women from the far north of the country. People scratched their heads to figure out why, all of a sudden, the women were so good.

Was it — *gasp!* — drugs?

None of the athletes ever tested positive for drugs, but they always seemed to miss drug tests and any competitions where testing officials showed up. Their coach, Ma Junren,

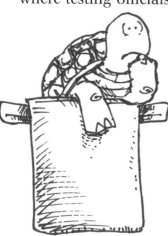

said they didn't need drugs; they had something better: soup and drinks made from turtle's blood and caterpillar fungus.

Many of the athletes eventually quit the national team, calling Ma's methods cruel.

His cooking certainly was. But people still wonder — was it really the soup?

EVENT #2
STRETCH YOUR CREDULITY

The record books are chock-full of impressive stats and stories.

But some of the results don't make sense. Every once in a while, you have to do a double take.

"That really happened?"

"That really happened?"

Yes!

Yes!

Here are some samples of the most unlikely, incredible, impossible, unbelievable wins.

Did they serve tea and crumpets in the penalty box?

Great Britain is not an ice-hockey powerhouse. But back in the 1930s, Britannia ruled the rink. Sort of.

A number of Canadians with British citizenship banded together to try to win some medals. They had their most amazing success in 1936. They beat Canada 2–1, Canada's first hockey loss at the Olympics. Then Britain beat the Czechs and tied the U.S. to claim the gold medal.

The team was finally defeated by a tougher enemy: the outbreak of World War Two. The British side won the war, but their hockey team has never made it to the Olympics since.

He tamed the Russian bear

One of the most stunning upsets in wrestling history happened on the mats in Sydney, Australia, in 2000. Russia's Alexander Karelin was the overwhelming favorite to win the super heavyweight division. Actually, "overwhelming" is an understatement: he'd won three Olympic gold medals in a row and was on a thirteen-year unbeaten streak. No one had even scored a point against him in ten years.

Rulon Gardner of the U.S. was certainly not the man to beat him. Gardner had never won a major title. But he figured he could at least play defensively and not let Karelin get a good grip on him.

Eventually, Karelin got so frustrated that he made a small mistake. Gardner saw his chance and scored a point. From then on, Gardner kept away from Karelin's grip and won 1–0. He became an instant star.

This Swahn was no spring chicken ... but Inge was barely hatched

Few people over forty compete at major sporting events, but Sweden's Oscar Swahn didn't even start winning medals until he was sixty.

That happened in 1908.

What's even more incredible is that Swahn continued to win medals for years. He won his last, a silver medal, when he was seventy-two.

At the 1920 Antwerp Olympics, Swahn was second in the running deer event. (Don't cry — competitors did not shoot real deer. They aimed at a cutout on a moving railcar.)

The flip side of the age coin was Denmark's Inge Sorensen. In 1936, she competed in the 200-meter breaststroke and won a bronze medal.

Sorensen was twelve years old, still the youngest individual medal winner in Olympic history.

The walk-on winner

Imagine heading out for vacation and coming home with a suitcase full of medals. That's exactly what Ireland's John Pius Boland did at the very first modern Olympic Games. He was visiting a friend in Greece in the summer of 1896, when the Games happened to be taking place.

Boland and his buddy had been playing some recreational tennis, and Boland was doing pretty well, so he decided to compete in the Games. He won the singles title and teamed up to win the doubles. After his holiday, he returned home to a successful career in politics.

Seeing double

The medal ceremony at the 1980 rowing venue in Moscow made the crowd do a double take.

Bernd and Jorg Landvoigt of East Germany were the defending champs. They were identical twins and rowed almost as one person. This made them an incredible force on the water.

But they were almost knocked off their pedestal by — what else? — another pair of identical twins: Yuri and Nikolai Pimenov of Russia. It was a close race between the pairs of twins, but the Landvoigt twins defended their title … and got identical gold medals. The Pimenovs got their identical silver medals.

Seeing double, again

When the Mahre twins, Phil and Steve, competed on the U.S. ski team, they would help each other out. After one finished a race, he would get on the radio, call up to his brother at the starting line and give him tips on how to go even faster.

And it worked. Phil won the gold and Steve the silver in the slalom at the 1984 games in Sarajevo.

Talk about brotherly love!

Putting the Soviets on ice

The Soviet Union was the undisputed master of international hockey for nearly forty years. It was knocked off the top spot only twice during that run, in 1960 and 1980, both times by the U.S.

The winning U.S. teams were a patchwork of minor-league players and unproven teenagers. No one gave them a chance. But they had the advantage of home ice — Squaw Valley in 1960 and Lake Placid in 1980 — and the crowd was with them.

Also, the goaltenders — Jack McCartan and Jim Craig — played the best hockey of their lives.

Here's a funky fact ...
The last player cut from the 1960 U.S. team was Herb Brooks. After he quit playing he became a coach. And guess who coached the 1980 gold-medal team? Yup, Herb Brooks.

She flipped, then flopped...

Lindsey Jacobellis of the U.S. had a huge lead in her snowboarding race in 2006.

Maybe she had too much of a lead, because, like the famous hare in the fable, she got a little cocky near the end.

On the final jump, just meters before the finish line, Jacobellis reached down and grabbed her board in the air, showing off with a little hot-dog move.

But she couldn't get the board back down quickly enough on the landing and she crashed.

Switzerland's Tanja Frieden passed her and won the gold medal.

Jacobellis got up as quickly as she could, but had to settle for second place.

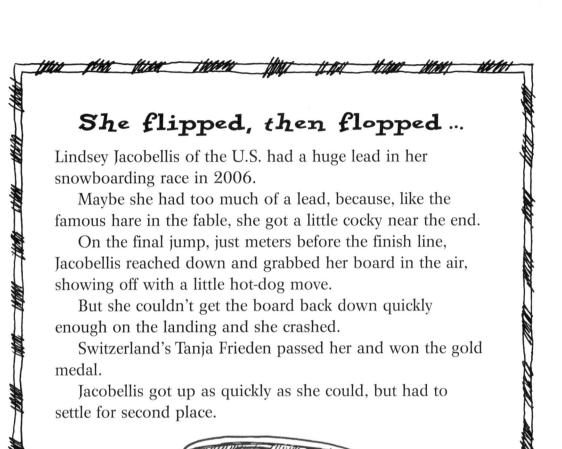

EVENT #3
CATCH A RIDE TO THE FINISH LINE!

FAMOUS CHEATS

The Olympics are supposed to be about fair play, but the athletes really, really want to win.

Sometimes they can't manage both. Think about it. A gold medal can be worth millions of dollars.

Would you cheat if it meant victory? Here are some people who said YES!

Race, then disgrace

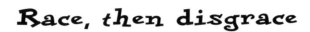

Canadian sprinter Ben Johnson won the 1988 Olympic 100-meter race in Seoul in 9.79 seconds, shattering the world record. How could he run so fast?

The answer came a few days after he'd been awarded the gold medal. Johnson tested positive for steroids. It was the first time a major champion had been caught taking a banned drug.

He claimed someone must have spiked his water bottle, but that excuse didn't fly. Johnson was stripped of the gold medal and banned from the sport for two years.

Johnson tried a comeback in the early 1990s, but he tested positive again and was banned for life.

Driver, take me to the finish line and step on it!

The marathon is one of the marquee events of the Games. People will do almost anything to win.

In 1904, Fred Lorz crossed the finish line in St. Louis first. He was even given a laurel wreath to celebrate. But guilt soon won out, and Lorz admitted the truth. He had developed cramps a few kilometers (miles) into the race, so he jumped into a car and hitched a ride most of the way.

He figured it would be funny to jump out near the finish line and win.

The officials didn't share his sense of humor. They stripped him of the win and awarded the victory to Thomas Hicks of the U.S., who'd actually run the whole race.

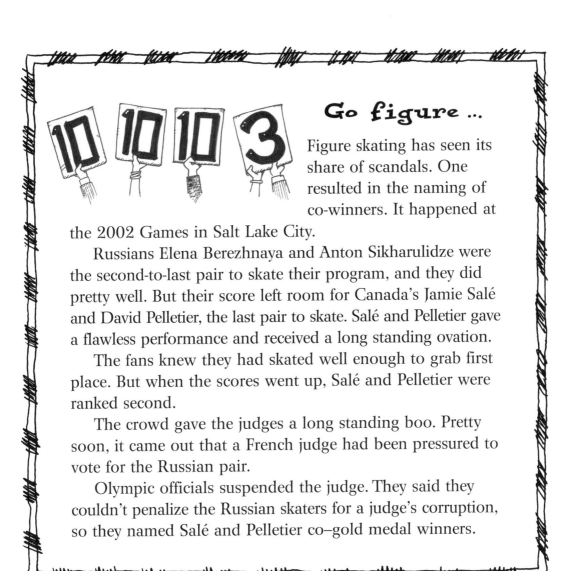

Go figure ...

Figure skating has seen its share of scandals. One resulted in the naming of co-winners. It happened at the 2002 Games in Salt Lake City.

Russians Elena Berezhnaya and Anton Sikharulidze were the second-to-last pair to skate their program, and they did pretty well. But their score left room for Canada's Jamie Salé and David Pelletier, the last pair to skate. Salé and Pelletier gave a flawless performance and received a long standing ovation.

The fans knew they had skated well enough to grab first place. But when the scores went up, Salé and Pelletier were ranked second.

The crowd gave the judges a long standing boo. Pretty soon, it came out that a French judge had been pressured to vote for the Russian pair.

Olympic officials suspended the judge. They said they couldn't penalize the Russian skaters for a judge's corruption, so they named Salé and Pelletier co–gold medal winners.

Down for the count!

The 1988 boxing finals in Seoul deserved the gold medal for "something fishy is going on here."

One South Korean boxer was so angry about losing a controversial decision that he sat down and refused to leave the ring for an hour.

A few days later, Roy Jones, Jr. of the U.S. clearly won a bout against another South Korean boxer, but the judges gave his opponent the win. Jones was shocked; so was just about everyone who'd watched the fight.

Maybe it was payback time for that earlier decision?

A few years later, evidence surfaced that Korean officials had bribed judges so that their boxer would win the second fight.

Vergüenza en usted!
(That's "shame on you" in Spanish!)

The Spanish basketball team won the gold medal at the 2000 Paralympics in Sydney, Australia, in the category for athletes with mental disabilities. One problem: most of the Spanish players didn't actually have mental disabilities — they were faking.

The story came to light when one member of the team felt guilty, returned his medal and squealed on his teammates.

Paralympic officials decided it was too difficult to enforce the rules, so they eliminated the mental-disabilities categories from future Paralympics. So the Spanish team really spoiled the Games for a lot of athletes.

Gracias amigos!

Quick, smudge some oil on your face

The 2004 Games were a success for Greece in many ways, but they started off with a major national embarrassment.

Runners Kostas Kenteris and Katerina Thanou were superstars and on almost all the posters and ads for the

Games. Then, right before the first day of the Games, the two didn't show up for their mandatory drug tests. A major no-no.

When they did surface, Kenteris and Thanou claimed they'd missed the tests because they'd been in a motorcycle accident. Problem was, police couldn't find any evidence of a crash. With their alibi gone bye-bye, the two eventually pulled out of the Games.

You stick that where? (The grossest thing you'll read in this book)

Anti-doping officials try to catch cheaters in a number of ways, especially by testing an athlete's urine. The athlete pees in a bottle; the officials then test the pee to see if it contains banned drugs.

So, how do you hide the evidence if you are taking drugs? Some athletes shoot clean pee up into their bladders.

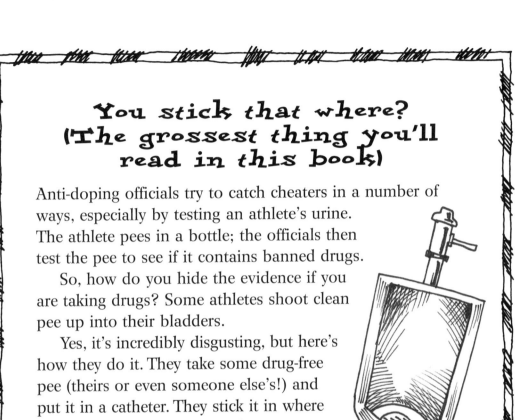

Yes, it's incredibly disgusting, but here's how they do it. They take some drug-free pee (theirs or even someone else's!) and put it in a catheter. They stick it in where the stuff usually comes out, then squeeze to keep it there. When it's time to fill the test bottle, they let the clean pee back out … the old-fashioned way.

Sometimes they even get away with it.

EVENT #4
BATTLING MOTHER NATURE!

Most sporting events are held outside. Sometimes fans say, "Ahh, the fresh air! Feel that cool breeze! Listen to those birds singing."

Other times it's more like, "AAAAAAAAAAAA!! Smog! Hurricane! Spewing lava!"

Make sure you're dressed in layers! Things can change fast!

The mountain moved the Games

The 1908 Olympic Games were supposed to be held in Italy, but the country's most famous volcano had other ideas. Just as the Italians were getting ready to build the facilities, Mount Vesuvius blew its top. And blew and blew. More than a hundred people died as lava, rock and ash bombarded nearby Naples.

The government looked at the damage and decided it needed to spend its money on something more important than a sporting event.

The Games moved to London.

Let it snow ... PLEASE!

The Winter Games are often plagued with weather problems. Skiing seems especially vulnerable. In 1932, organizers in Lake Placid, New York, had to truck in snow from Canada to cover the cross-country course.

For the alpine events in 1998 in Nagano, Japan, it rained or was foggy throughout most of the Games. Officials worked and re-worked the schedules. They even considered canceling some events. Eventually they crammed them into the last few days of competition, when the weather improved — slightly.

In Calgary in 1988, the problem was wind. Organizers had been warned to install windscreens, but didn't. High winds knocked over skiers and spectators and forced a number of postponements.

Why are the lifeguard's lips blue?

Sometimes the Games can be too cold.

The 1896 Athens Olympics featured swimming events in the Aegean Sea. Swimmers were rowed out into a bay, then dumped into the water. First back to shore was the winner. This would have been fine in summer, but it was April, and the water was freezing.

Hungarian swimmer Alfred Hajos claimed that his will to live took over. (He knew what he was talking about: he learned to swim after his father drowned in the Danube River.)

His "AHHHH! I don't want to die!" strategy worked. So did smothering himself with grease to keep warm in the water. Hajos won the 1200-meter race.

Here's a funky fact ... Hajos even won medals when he wasn't an athlete, taking the silver medal for architecture at the 1924 Games!

Peak performances

Olympics have been held in some of the highest places in the world, like the Mexico City Games in 1968. As the city is almost a mile and a half (2 kilometers) above sea level, athletes worried that the thin air would hamper their performances.

No way. In fact, records fell like crazy, especially in the track events. The most dramatic example of the wonders of thin air was the performance of American long-jumper Bob Beamon. He jumped forward more than 29 feet (8.8 meters), beating the previous record by about 2 feet (0.6 meters)!

That water has bite

The swimming portion of the 2000 triathlon was held in Sydney Harbour, where it's not uncommon to see sharks swimming among the boats. One triathlete even worried that he would be in danger because his wetsuit made him look a lot like a seal.

Sydney organizers did their best to make everyone feel at ease. They even sent divers into the harbor wearing special sonar suits to scare sharks away.

No one saw a shark or got bitten — but, man, did they swim fast.

Maybe they should wear swimsuits with their skates

Sometimes Olympic organizers are just asking for trouble. Ice hockey made its debut at the 1920 Games.

In Antwerp.

In April.

The games were originally going to take place on the Brussels canal, but organizers wised up and moved hockey indoors to the Antwerp Ice Palace. The Winnipeg Falcons won the gold medal for Canada.

After that, Olympic competitions were divided into Summer and Winter Games — much better for ice hockey.

EVENT #5
HEROES
(TRY NOT TO CRY)

Here are some of the real heroes we mentioned.

Many athletes have won medals and championships, but some are winners for what they've had to overcome. Others haven't won medals at all, but did win the respect of their competitors and the fans.

I'm starting to get all weepy — we'd better move through this event quickly.

Finally!

American speedskater Dan Jansen had to battle repeated tragedy and bad luck.

He was unbeatable as he prepared for the 1988 Games. But on the day of his race, his sister died from leukemia. Jansen stumbled and finished out of the medals. He fell again during his next race, two days later.

In 1992, Jansen was again favored to win. Instead, he stumbled and fell. In 1994, Jansen was no longer a favorite, so no one was surprised when he stumbled in the 500-meter race and finished eighth.

He had one chance left in his career, the 1000-meter race just days later. This race was not his specialty, but he broke into a quick lead and was well out in front when he stumbled again. But this time, Jansen kept his balance and finished in first place. He cried as he skated a victory lap, holding his daughter Jane, named after the sister who'd died before Dan's first Olympic race six years earlier.

The loser was a real winner

Athletes will often do anything to win a medal. Then there's Larry Lemieux. In 1988, the Canadian sailor gave up his chance at a medal to save two lives.

Lemieux was headed for a top finish in the Finn class. Then, near the end of the race, he saw a boat capsize in the

 rough water, sending two of his competitors into the drink. Lemieux didn't hesitate. He abandoned the race and sailed over to save the men — a dangerous maneuver in the huge waves.

Lemieux didn't win a sailing medal, but Olympic President Juan Antonio Samaranch awarded him a special medal for bravery.

Ouch! We (ouch) won! (ouch)

The final of the 1996 gymnastics competition in Atlanta was a real nail-biter — and leg-cruncher.

The U.S. had a narrow lead over Russia. All they needed was for Kerri Strug to land an almost perfect final vault jump to clinch the win. One problem: Strug had fallen on her first jump and torn two ligaments in her ankle. She could barely walk.

Instead, she ran, vaulted and landed, standing still until the judges registered her landing. Then she collapsed in excruciating pain.

Her coach had to carry her to the medal ceremony, but she was all smiles when she received the gold along with her teammates.

This one's for you, Dad

American Bill Havens knew all about sacrifice. He was favored to win a medal in rowing at the 1924 Paris Olympics. Given how slow trans-Atlantic crossings were back then, he decided to skip the event to stay home with his very pregnant wife. Soon after the Games, their son, Frank, was born.

In 1952, Frank Havens made the Olympic team in canoeing. After his race, Frank sent Bill this telegram: "Dear Dad. Thanks for waiting around for me to be born. I'm coming home with your gold medal. Your loving son, Frank."

Frank had won the 10 000-meter event.

Norway did it the right way

The cross-country races at the 2006 Games in Turin, Italy, were incredibly close.

Canada's Sara Renner was leading the relay race when one of her ski poles broke. She was falling behind quickly, when a man on the sidelines handed her a new pole. Renner and her partner Beckie Scott finished in second place.

Who was the kind man?

Norwegian coach Bjornar Haakensmoen. Norway finished fourth.

Some people criticized Haakensmoen for helping another country finish ahead of Norway. But he said the Olympics are about fair play, not just winning medals.

He also told Renner she could keep the pole as a souvenir.

What a guy!

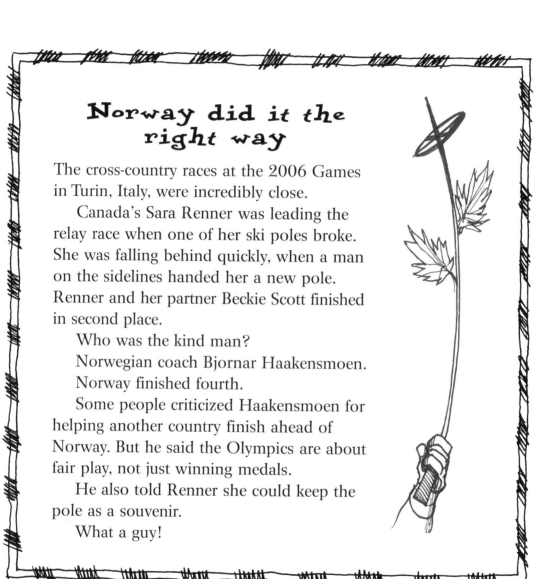

Koss is the boss

Norway's Johann Olav Koss was the undisputed hero of the 1994 Olympics, setting numerous world speedskating records on his home rink in Lillehammer.

Many athletes use their fame to earn a living. Koss wanted to do more. He donated his prize money to Olympic Aid, a charity developed by the Lillehammer organizing committee to support people in war-torn countries and areas of distress. Right after the Olympics, Koss became an ambassador for the charity and visited numerous countries in Africa.

He was so moved that he decided to work for the charity full-time. Eventually he became its head. The charity is now called "Right to Play." It has since raised millions of dollars and helped bring sports training and equipment to the poor of Africa.

Many athletes have become huge supporters of the group. Speedskaters Clara Hughes and Joey Cheek donated tens of thousands of dollars each after winning races at the 2006 Games.

EVENT #6
DODGE THE AMMUNITION AND FALLING BIRDS ...

The Olympic Games you watch on TV today are a lot different than those of a hundred years ago. Back then it wasn't just running, jumping and swimming.

We're going to head back in time to before TV existed, when the Olympics also included such things as live-animal hunting and dueling with pistols.

Maybe some of these should get a second chance at being official events. Others definitely should not.

What the heck is "plunging"?

Well, plunging is, or was, a lot like it sounds: you plunged into the water.

The plungers would stand on the side of a pool and dive in; then they'd hold their breath and glide underwater as far as possible. Longest glide without a breath won.

You're right — not very exciting, as folks discovered after it was part of the 1904 Games in St. Louis. The diving-into-the-water part was obviously the best bit and became an official sport at the next Olympics.

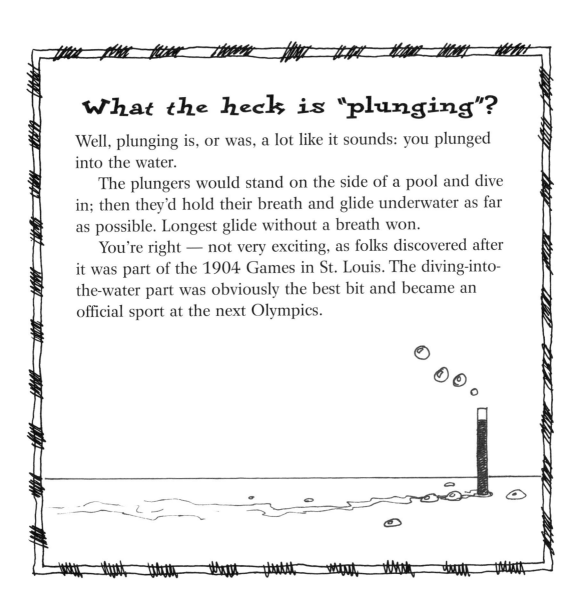

It was a real tug-of-war

Tug-of-war was part of the ancient Games, debuting around about three thousand years ago. And it hasn't changed much. Two teams of men pull on a rope, trying to drag the other group over a line.

So it was no surprise that it found its way into the early modern games.

But even something this simple can be controversial. In 1908, a group of English policemen successfully tugged the U.S. team in mere seconds. The U.S. accused the English of using illegal shoes. Officials disagreed.

The U.S. walked off the field in a huff and refused to participate in any more matches. Teams from Great Britain won all three medals.

Pigeon shooting

Yes, competitors actually shot and killed pigeons at the 1900 Olympics in Paris. The pigeons were released in front of the contestants, then they opened fire.

Bang.

Bang.

Bang.

The more birds killed, the better. Belgium's Leon de Lunden won by killing twenty-one unlucky birds.

The event was never held again, as it proved not only violent but also incredibly messy.

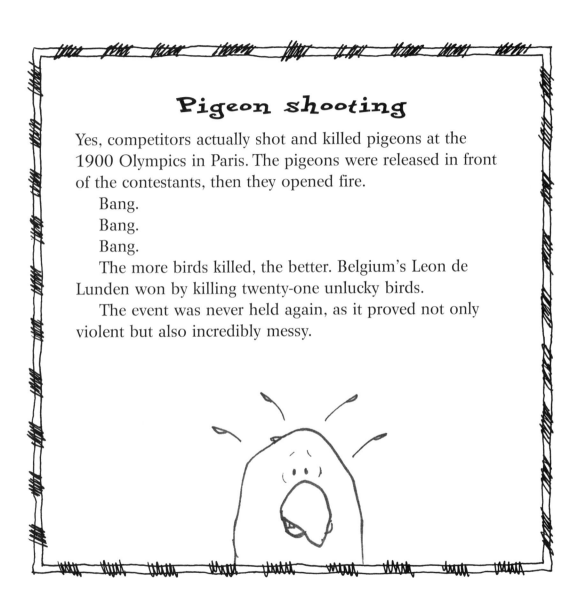

People shooting?
And clubbing?

"Pistol dueling" made its way into the 1906 Athens Games.
Luckily, the duelers didn't actually shoot at each other, but at elegant dummies wearing frock coats and big bull's-eyes on their chests. Weird. Kind of like blasting holes in a store mannequin.

The "club swinging" event at the 1904 and 1932 Olympics

also sounded more dangerous than it was. Contestants did not swing clubs at each other. Instead, they twirled a club and ribbons around their heads. Most stylish won.

EVENT #7
RUN AND TAKE THE MONEY

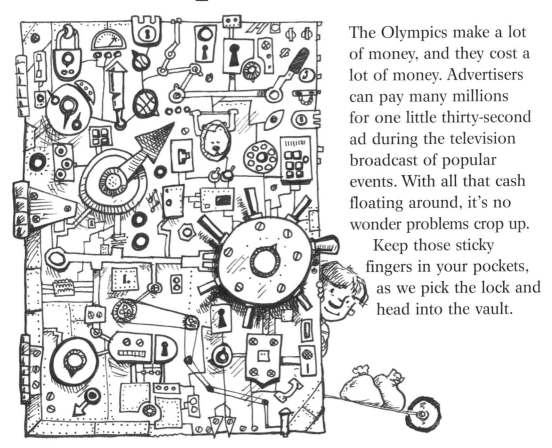

The Olympics make a lot of money, and they cost a lot of money. Advertisers can pay many millions for one little thirty-second ad during the television broadcast of popular events. With all that cash floating around, it's no wonder problems crop up.

Keep those sticky fingers in your pockets, as we pick the lock and head into the vault.

I hope that includes the tip!

Hosting an Olympics can bring a lot of good things to a city: prestige, tourism, better streets, subways and, of course, sports facilities. But it can also bring a heap of debt.

As the bills started rolling in for the 1976 Games in Montreal, people got worried. Things were costing a lot more than they had expected. Montreal mayor Jean Drapeau tried to reassure them, claiming that, "The Olympics can no more lose money than a man can have a baby."

No one's sure if he actually gave birth, but he certainly laid an egg. Montreal ended up more than a billion dollars in the red and took thirty years to pay it off.

No wonder there are so many ads

The Olympics are a TV-ratings bonanza. Hundreds of millions of people tune in to cheer on their country's athletes. With all those viewers, no wonder the money that networks pay for the right to broadcast the Games is downright mind-boggling.

The NBC TV network really wanted to be the official U.S. Olympic broadcaster and happily paid the International Olympic Committee nearly six billion dollars U.S. for broadcast rights to all the Games from 2000 to 2012. That's about a billion dollars for each Games! And twenty bucks for every man, woman or child in the country!

They make that money back by selling ads — and, man, do they sell. Ads during the opening ceremonies alone bring in as much as thirty million dollars.

If you're a pro you've got to go

For its first hundred years or so, the modern Olympic movement was strictly amateur: if you got paid to play a sport, you couldn't compete in the Games. A good idea, but only people who already had money could afford to compete for the love of it.

Jim Thorpe was the first big victim of this irony. He was an amazing all-around athlete. In 1912, he won both the decathlon and the pentathlon in Stockholm; but, a year later, it was discovered that he had once accepted a few dollars to play baseball. Thorpe admitted it, but pointed out that he was a poor Native-American kid who needed the money.

Too bad, said Olympic officials. He was declared a professional and was stripped of his medals. Thorpe went on to a brilliant career in professional football, but his Olympic disappointment always rankled. Thirty years after his death, Olympic officials overturned their ruling and presented Thorpe's children with replacement medals.

EVENT #8
RUN INTO
YESTERDAY

Time for some *real* time travel.

We're heading back about three thousand years. That's when the first Olympic Games were held.

No high-tech sneakers and TV coverage.

Just a bunch of athletes meeting every few years to see who was the strongest, bravest and, sometimes, meanest.

Hey, I can see your butt

Athletes in the ancient Olympics often competed in the buff. Why? Maybe the Greeks just liked being naked. (Think of all the nude guys on those Greek vases you see in museums.)

But one story has it that a runner once lost his loincloth during a race, tripped on it and lost. After that, runners decided clothes were risky.

A variation of this theory claims that the runner who lost his loincloth went on to win, as he was not slowed down by bulky undies.

You choose which version you like.

Pankration

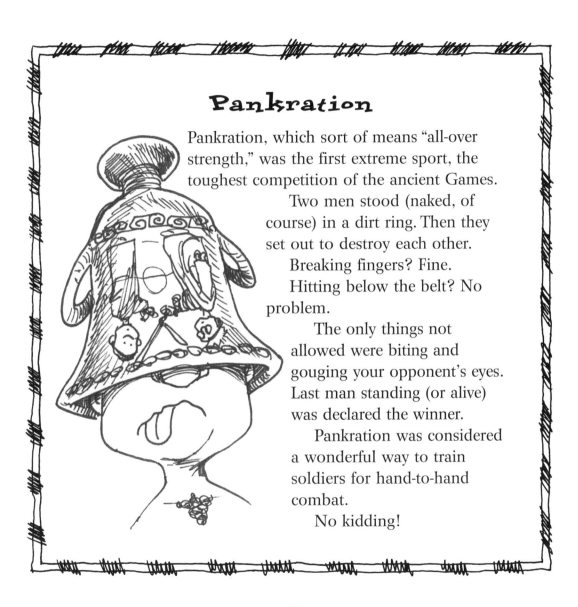

Pankration, which sort of means "all-over strength," was the first extreme sport, the toughest competition of the ancient Games.

Two men stood (naked, of course) in a dirt ring. Then they set out to destroy each other.

Breaking fingers? Fine.

Hitting below the belt? No problem.

The only things not allowed were biting and gouging your opponent's eyes. Last man standing (or alive) was declared the winner.

Pankration was considered a wonderful way to train soldiers for hand-to-hand combat.

No kidding!

I'm not telling him he finished second

The Greeks created the Games, but the Romans kept them going, right up until about 300 AD. They were such enthusiasts that even the emperors got involved. That was not always a good thing.

The emperor Nero was famous as one of the cruellest dictators in history. He may have set fire to Rome so he could rebuild it more to his liking. He had a similar "me-first" attitude toward sports. In 67 AD, he fell out of his chariot during a race, but paid the judges to declare him the winner. (You can't really blame them. People who didn't humor Nero tended to end up dead.) Nero went on to "win" six events, but was run out of his job a year later by rebel mobs.

Green, not gold

There were actually no medals handed out at the ancient Olympics. Victorious athletes were crowned with a wreath of olive branches, and that was about it.

Of course, there were perks. The athlete's hometown would often erect statues and provide him with free food for life. Some famous athletes even found their way into poems you can still read today (if you can read ancient Greek).

In a nice twist, organizers of the 2004 Games in Athens combined old and new. They awarded winners olive wreaths along with their gold medals.

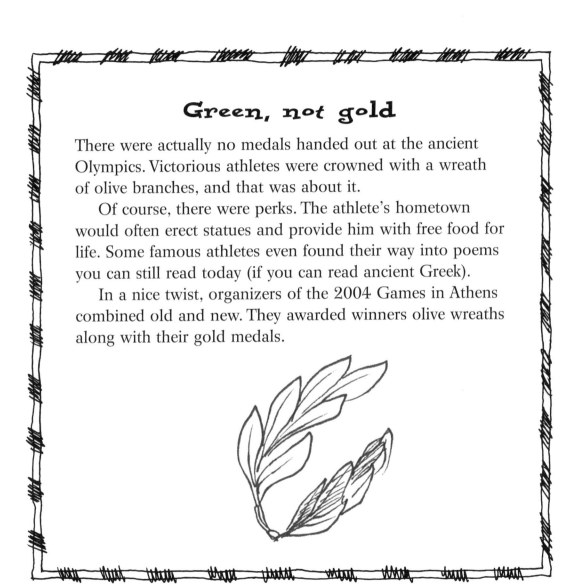

Can't bury the past

Athens went all out to recapture some of its old glory when it was awarded the 2004 Games. Olympia, the site of the ancient Olympics (and the modern shot put event), was incredibly well preserved: it had spent hundreds of years under volcanic ash.

But all that history caused problems as well. Almost every time construction crews started digging, they uncovered an ancient statue or temple. Then work had to be halted until historians and archaeologists had secured the ruins. That took time, and time was running out. Games organizers scrambled right up until the last second to get the city ready.

EVENT #9
STAY ON YOUR BUTTS AND IN THOSE SEATS!

A couple of thousand athletes usually compete at each Olympics.

They are allowed to be on the fields and rinks and tracks.

Fans are supposed to sit and watch.

But sometimes the fans want to get in on the act as well.

And that's almost always a bad idea.

Marathon moron

The 2004 Athens marathon had a weird, and unfortunate, end.

Brazil's Vanderlei de Lima had the lead with just a few miles to go, when a fan jumped from the crowd and tackled him! The fan was wearing a protest sign. Police say he was also drunk.

Other fans fought off the loony, but by then de Lima had lost his lead. Miraculously, he was able to regain his footing and continue the race. He ended up third. Italy's Stefano Baldini won the gold medal.

News of the attack quickly reached the stadium, where fans waited at the finish line.

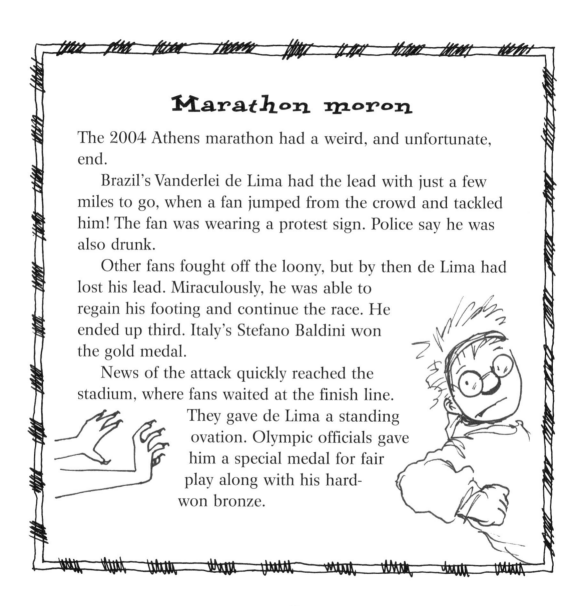

They gave de Lima a standing ovation. Olympic officials gave him a special medal for fair play along with his hard-won bronze.

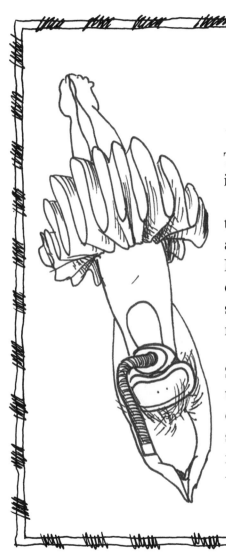

That's the stupidest bathing suit I've ever seen

There was another case of fan lunacy in Athens — at the diving competition.

A Canadian man dressed in a tutu jumped onto the diving board and into the water. He had the Internet address of a casino painted on his back. He was arrested, but his silliness actually helped the host nation win its first gold medal.

The Greek divers Bimis and Sirandis had a surprising lead in their event, but there were better divers to follow. The tutu incident seemed to shake up their rivals, many of whom had poor dives, and the Greeks celebrated gold.

Pop, I heard a "POP"

Britain's Derek Redmond got help from a special fan when he needed it most.

Redmond was favored to win the 400-meter race at the Barcelona Games in 1992 and had an early lead in his semi-final. Then he heard a "pop" in his leg. He'd torn his hamstring.

Screaming in pain, he fell to the track. Medics rushed over to put Redmond on a stretcher. He refused, stood up and tried to hobble to the finish line.

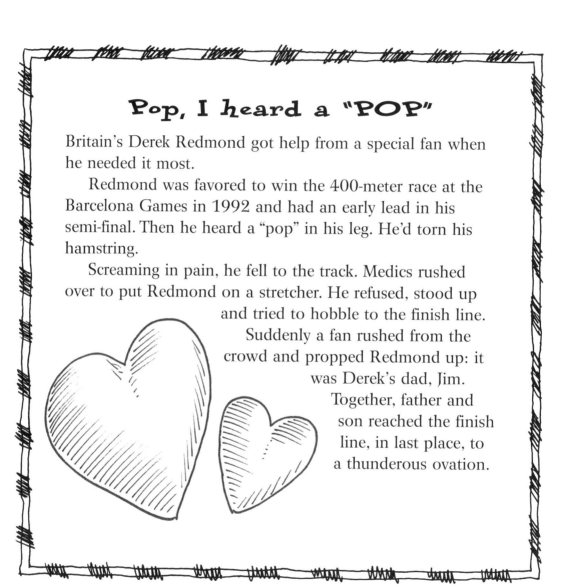

Suddenly a fan rushed from the crowd and propped Redmond up: it was Derek's dad, Jim. Together, father and son reached the finish line, in last place, to a thunderous ovation.

Who knew one second could last so loooooooooooong?

The U.S. basketball team was sure the referee in the 1972 final was also a fan … of the Soviet Union.

The U.S. had a one-point lead with one second left. The Soviets missed on their last shot, and the U.S. players celebrated.

But the referee said, "Nope, the play didn't count." He said the clock had to be reset.

The Soviets tried again and didn't score. Incredibly, the referee reset the clock again and gave them yet another chance.

The third time, the Soviets finally sunk a basket to win the game.

The U.S. protested and refused to accept their silver medals.

Booooooooooooooooooooooooooo

Sometimes the fans can shut down a whole competition.

The 2004 gymnastics competition in Athens was packed every night — and the fans knew their stuff. During the men's final, Russia's Alexei Nemov received ridiculously low marks.

The fans booed. And booed. And booed. Officials asked for quiet. The crowd got louder. Finally, the judges changed their scores, admitting their mistake.

Or maybe they were just trying to get the folks to shut up.

Turin around ...

Security was everywhere at the 2006 Olympic Games in Turin. But somehow there were several security breaches.

Once, a streaker ran onto the ice at the curling venue. Luckily for the fans, he was covering up his private parts with a rubber chicken.

Then, at the very end of the Games, at the closing ceremonies, another streaker tried to crash the stage. Police stopped her.

But a few minutes later, a man ran on stage during a speech. He grabbed the microphone and yelled, "Passion Lives Here," the slogan for the Games. He was immediately grabbed by security officers.

Police say he had been wearing an official uniform and blended into the crowd on the side of the stage.

EVENT #10
GET THE BANDAGES READY!

OUCH!

Injuries are common in sports. (Just look at the hurdles you have to clear, the javelins and shot puts you have to dodge.)

But some injuries are truly uncommon — and uncommonly painful.

And, somehow, the athletes can compete through the pain.

There's a saying in sports: "No pain, no gain."

You might gain some chuckles and inspiration from this chapter.

Whack!

Greg Louganis was the greatest diver of his era, but he almost didn't survive the 1988 Seoul Games.

Louganis was completing his preliminary dives when he spun too close to the board and hit it. He fell into the water, bleeding from a gash on his head. Medical staff hauled him out of the pool and quickly closed the cut with temporary sutures.

Louganis was in pain, but continued his dives and qualified for the final. He paid a quick visit to the hospital to get some proper stitches, then returned to win the gold medal.

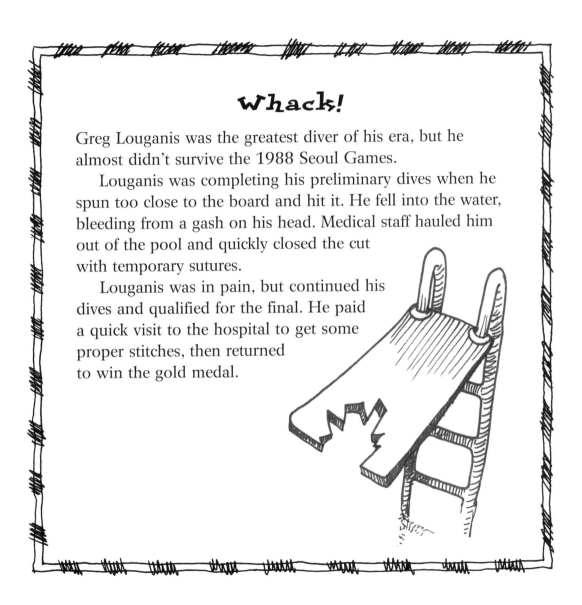

Frost bites

American Rulon Gardner won gold in wrestling in Sydney in 2000 and was looking forward to defending the title four years later in Athens. But his training took a major detour one winter night.

Gardner was out on his snowmobile when he got stuck in some deep snow. He spent an entire night in the freezing  cold before rescuers found him. Doctors were amazed he hadn't died, although he did suffer frostbite, and they had to remove one of his toes.

Gardner recovered, but his balance was thrown right off. He had to change his wrestling style completely to accommodate the missing toe.

Gardner did make it to Athens and won a bronze medal.

Saddled with pain

In equestrian events it's often the horses that risk injury, but Australian rider Bill Roycroft battled through pain to win in 1960.

Although he and his horse crashed during the cross-country portion of his three-day event, Roycroft got back in the saddle and finished the race. Then he was rushed to hospital. Doctors told him he was done — he had a broken collarbone and a concussion.

But if he didn't race again, his team would forfeit.

No way Roycroft was going to let that happen. He signed himself out of the hospital and headed to the show-jumping venue. His teammates had to help him into the saddle — he could barely move.

Somehow he rode a flawless performance, and Australia won the gold medal.

I'm sorry but if you're a little horse you can't come in

The 1956 equestrian events weren't held up by injury, but by illness, even though no one was sick.

Australia hosted the Games and has very strict laws about letting animals into the country. Australia is an island, and once an animal disease comes ashore, it's hard to get rid of because the local critters have no resistance to it. So Australia demands that all horses spend six months in quarantine before they're let loose down under.

But the competitors' horses needed to be competing and practicing right up until the Games started, so the riders said, "No way."

Australia replied, "Okay, no horses."

So while the rest of the Olympics were held in Melbourne, the equestrian events were held thousands of miles away, in Sweden.

Silken steel

Canadian Silken Laumann was competing in a rowing regatta weeks before the 1992 Olympics in Barcelona, when a German boat rammed into her. The boat crushed a bone in her leg and left fragments of wood embedded in her muscle.

So, did Laumann quit? Not a chance. She had back-to-back-to-back operations to repair the damage. As soon as she could, she got back in her boat, desperately trying to build up her muscles in time for the Games. She made it, with her leg heavily bandaged.

Laumann finished third in her race, possibly the most celebrated bronze medal in history.

EVENT #11
TRY NOT TO
KILL YOURSELF...

Olympians are a collection of the greatest and most talented athletes in the world.

For the most part.

But every once in a while, an athlete qualifies for the Olympics who would probably have been better off staying in bed.

Forget about competing for a medal, this bunch is just trying to survive.

Throw him a life jacket

Eric Moussambani made history at the 2000 Sydney Olympics by not drowning.

He was competing in the 100-meter freestyle swim race — a short distance for most swimmers, but it took Moussambani forever. This wasn't too surprising. Moussambani is from Equatorial Guinea, a country with no lakes and few pools.

He'd taken up swimming only a few months before the Olympics. As he flailed and splashed around, lifeguards were positioned on the pool deck in case he went under.

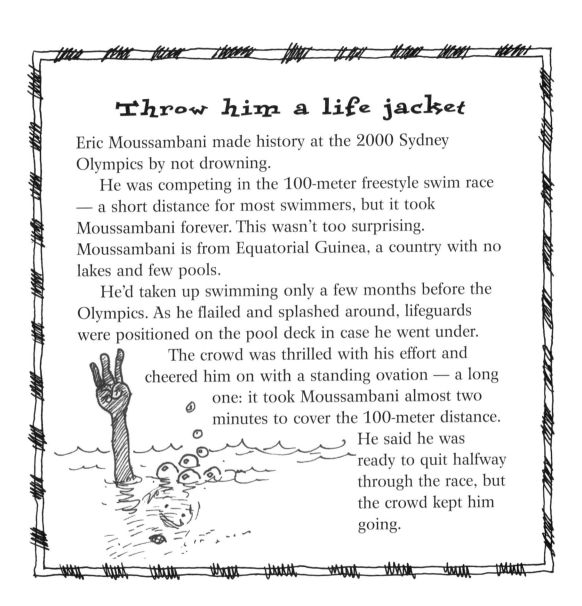

The crowd was thrilled with his effort and cheered him on with a standing ovation — a long one: it took Moussambani almost two minutes to cover the 100-meter distance. He said he was ready to quit halfway through the race, but the crowd kept him going.

Kenya ski as well as run?

Kenya is known for its great cross-country runners. (There's lots of country to cross and it's warm year-round.) Mike Boit was one of the country's best and had won a number of medals.

Mike's younger brother, Philip, decided he wanted to compete, too — but at the *Winter Games*. So, in 1998, he lined up for the 10-kilometer cross-country ski race.

He finished well back — way, way back — but caught the attention of the world's greatest skier, Norway's Bjorn Daehlie, who'd won the race but waited at the finish line to greet Boit with a huge hug.

It was the beginning of a beautiful friendship. Boit even named his son Bjorn.

Reggae beaten

The Jamaican bobsled team was the hit of the 1988 Calgary Games — a bit of a surprise given that Jamaica has no winter to speak of, and few mountains.

Bobsled races start with sprinters pushing the sled at top speed. Now, Jamaica has lots of sprinters, so they figured they could get a fast start and then just hope to get to the bottom of the run in one piece.

They started training by pushing a cart down a dirt hill in the Jamaican bush. After months of practice, they figured 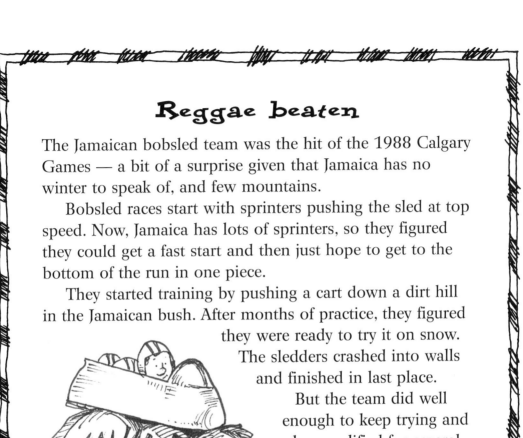 they were ready to try it on snow. The sledders crashed into walls and finished in last place.

But the team did well enough to keep trying and has qualified for several Winter Games since.

Propped up

Dorando Pietri of Italy became a star for *losing* the 1908 marathon. Pietri entered the London stadium first. But then he staggered, turned back and collapsed just before the finish line. The crowd tried to cheer him on, track-side officials helped him up, but he kept falling. Finally, they walked him the final few meters and declared him the winner.

By this time, Johnny Hayes of the U.S. was entering the stadium and soon crossed the finish line under his own steam. Pietri's win was protested by other teams — they even got into a fistfight over it. Officials relented and Hayes was named the winner.

But it's Pietri we remember. He became a folk hero. In London, Queen Alexandra awarded him a gold cup for perseverance. He even had a popular song written about him.

EVENT #12
PUT A SHIRT ON!
WARDROBE MALFUNCTIONS

Clothes are a big part of the Olympics.

Sports teams spend millions of dollars on equipment to try to gain a competitive advantage.

Countries also vie for the best-looking (and, thus, highest-selling) uniforms.

But some clothes should definitely have stayed on the rack.

Get a look at that

Canadian triathlete Simon Whitfield turned heads at the 2000 Sydney Olympics. It wasn't just that he was first, but that he crossed the finish line bare chested.

He wasn't trying to be macho. Whitfield said his uniform was sent to him in the mail, and it was the wrong size, but there was no time to get another one. He stuffed himself into the extra-small suit, but it shrank even more after the swimming portion of the race.

Whitfield couldn't keep it zipped up, so he competed with a little extra breeze on his pectorals.

He had no trouble getting the right size after winning the gold medal.

Me Tarzan ...
you lose

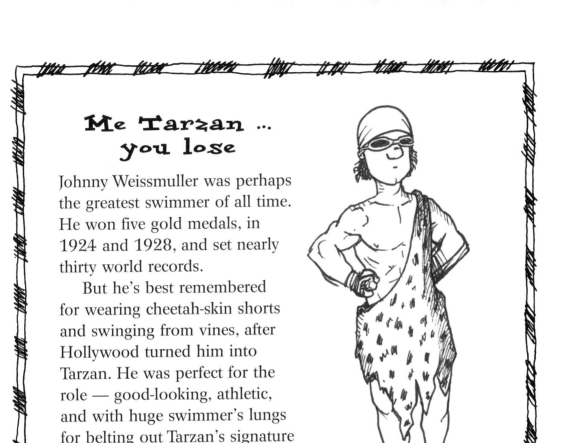

Johnny Weissmuller was perhaps the greatest swimmer of all time. He won five gold medals, in 1924 and 1928, and set nearly thirty world records.

But he's best remembered for wearing cheetah-skin shorts and swinging from vines, after Hollywood turned him into Tarzan. He was perfect for the role — good-looking, athletic, and with huge swimmer's lungs for belting out Tarzan's signature "Ahhhhahahhhhhahahhhhhh."

Weissmuller made twelve Tarzan movies. You can still catch some on late-night TV.

Do these make me look fast?

Athletes are always looking for ways to move faster. They come up with new suits, fibers, helmets — whatever can shave a few seconds or even milliseconds off their times.

One of the first breakthroughs came in 1962. Speedskaters competed in warm, heavy clothes until Canadian Paul Enock tried something lighter and smoother. He was training for the upcoming Olympics and wasn't happy with his times. He borrowed his wife's nylon panty hose and broke the world record in them.

Pretty soon, everyone was wearing sleeker fabrics.

Maybe *that's* a *good thing* ...

Imagine sitting on a sled, heading face-first down an icy track at 100-kilometers an hour ... and not being able to see where you're going!

Canada's Melissa Hollingsworth-Richards is one of the best skeleton racers in the world.

She was getting ready for the 2006 Games in Turin and was trying out a new racing suit.

Just as she started her race, the hood of the suit slid down over her eyes. Incredibly, she felt her way through the icy fast course, relying on her memory of its curves and twists. And won!

Hollingsworth-Richards joked that she had raced with "blinding speed."

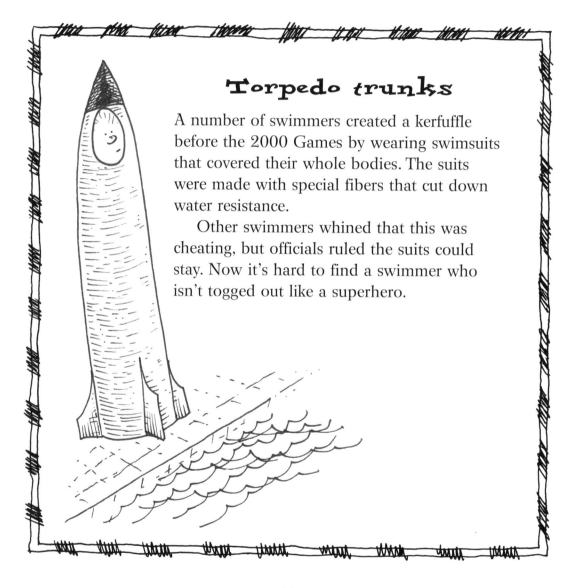

Torpedo trunks

A number of swimmers created a kerfuffle before the 2000 Games by wearing swimsuits that covered their whole bodies. The suits were made with special fibers that cut down water resistance.

Other swimmers whined that this was cheating, but officials ruled the suits could stay. Now it's hard to find a swimmer who isn't togged out like a superhero.

Cut short

Cuba's Felix Carvajal showed up for the 1904 marathon final in long pants and street shoes. He'd lost all his belongings gambling while en route to the Olympics.

Officials delayed the start of the race while Carvajal borrowed some scissors and cut off his pant legs.

He was leading for most of the race — until he spotted an apple orchard and stepped off the course for a snack. Problem was, the apples were green. He got cramps near the end of the race and finished fourth.

Ski whiz ...

Canada's Jeff Bean was practicing for the aerials event in Turin when his equipment let him down.

He had just launched himself in the air on one of the big jumps, when his skis flew off.

Both of them.

Bean spun in the air, twisting and turning and, miraculously, landed the  jump on his butt. That sounds painful, but Bean says it saved him from a nasty knee injury.

In fact, he says the scariest part was when the skis almost hit him as he flew in the air.

He was able to compete the next day.

He made extra sure that his skis were on tightly.

EVENT #13
CLEAR THE TRACK! HERE COME THE POLITICIANS

Part of the Olympics is bringing together athletes from different countries.

The goal is to share their cultures and ideas through sport.

Nice idea, but sometimes those countries don't like each other very much, and that can create … tension.

Why is the water red?

The Soviet Union invaded Hungary shortly before the 1956 Games in Melbourne. The Hungarians decided to fight back. Their weapon? Water polo.

They grabbed, clutched and scratched at the Soviet players and took a quick 4–0 lead. Then one of the Hungarian players was hit in the head by a Soviet player. He bled so much the water turned red.

Police were called in to prevent the fans (most cheering for Hungary) from rioting.

They called the match before things got totally out of hand. Hungary won the gold medal.

Slam dunk

In a last-second decision, many African nations boycotted the 1976 Summer Games. (They were angry because the New Zealand rugby team had toured South Africa — apartheid was still in place — and New Zealand was going to compete in Montreal.)

How last-second was it?

Well, Italy showed up for its first basketball game against Egypt. Egypt pulled out right before the game and didn't show up.

The Italian team lined up for the opening tip-off. They got the ball (surprise, surprise) and scored.

That gave them the official win, 2-0 — probably the lowest-scoring basketball game ever.

Dictator schmiktator

Adolf Hitler wanted to use the 1936 Games in Munich to advance his warped view of society. But two athletes upstaged him: Jesse Owens of the U.S. and Luz Long of Germany.

Owens was having trouble; he was fouling out on the long jump. Long advised him to leap well before the foul line, and he would still have no trouble making the final. He even offered to mark the right spot with his towel.

Owens was hugely impressed by Long's bravery. He said he was shocked that Long would risk helping a black athlete from the U.S. with Hitler watching from the stands. Yet he took Long's advice, made the final and won — his second of four gold medals in Munich.

Hitler wasn't impressed. He didn't stick around for the medal ceremony.

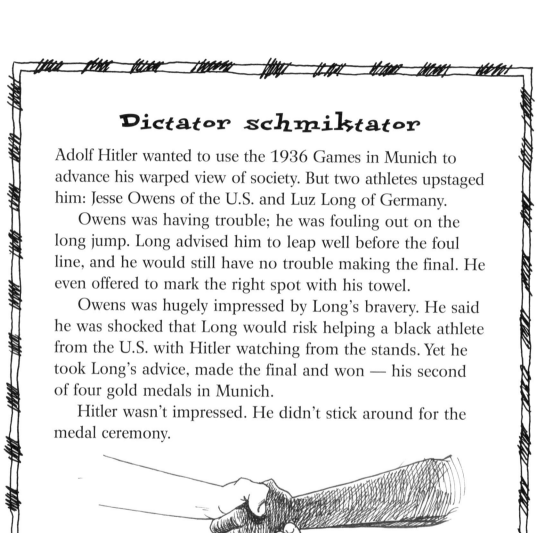

Stop shooting, we're trying to run here

The ancient Olympics grew so popular that warring states would stop fighting when the Games were on. The truce was long enough to give all the athletes time to get to the Games, compete and return home.

Olympic officials have tried to suggest similar truces in modern times. So far? No luck.

Your medal, your Highness

Many members of royalty have taken time from their busy lives to become Olympic athletes.

Alexander the Great's dad, Philip II of Macedon, won three equestrian medals at the ancient Games. He celebrated by stamping his victories on the kingdom's coins.

Prince Albert of Monaco competed in bobsledding in five Olympics, but didn't win any medals. No celebratory coins from him.

Great Britain's Princess Anne competed in show jumping at a number of Olympics. At the 1976 Games, she crashed and was motionless on the ground for five minutes. But she recovered and completed her event.

Here's a funky fact … Princess Anne likes the Olympics so much, she helped London win the right to host the 2012 Games.

Hey! Put that back!

Australian swimmer Dawn Fraser won tons of medals, but her career came to an abrupt end at the Tokyo Olympics in 1964, when she pulled a stunt that nearly caused an international incident.

Fraser was celebrating yet another gold medal. Maybe she was celebrating a little too much. She climbed a flagpole at the Imperial Palace and stole the Japanese flag. She was arrested at the scene by police, but when they recognized her, they dropped all charges. The Emperor even let her keep the flag as a souvenir.

Australian sports officials were not amused. They banned Fraser for ten years, ending her career but increasing her popularity. She was later elected to state parliament.

EVENT #14
STUMBLING AND FUMBLING TO THE TOP

There's a lot of pressure to get everything right at the Olympics. Not just on athletes, but judges, TV crews — everyone. Sometimes, things get seriously messed up.

Other times, things get a little messed up, and then have happy endings. Here are some people who turned tragedy into victory.

Two left thumbs cost her the gold

Canadian Sylvie Frechette was sure she'd won the synchro swimming title in 1992, and she had. But a misplaced finger cost her the title, at least for a while.

One judge meant to give Frechette a big score, but pressed the wrong button on her scoring pad. Frechette ended up second. Canadian officials protested.

It took more than a year, but Olympic officials finally agreed that Frechette shouldn't suffer because of someone else's mistake.

They named her a co-winner and gave her a duplicate gold medal.

Scaling back

Wrestlers watch their weight very, very carefully. (They have to. One gram over your weight category and you're out.) Many will starve or even dehydrate themselves to stay below their weight limit.

U.S. wrestler Charles Vinci weighed himself just fifteen minutes before the official weigh-in at the 1956 Melbourne Olympics. He was 200 grams over his limit. That's less than half a pound.

How do you lose weight when it's too late to diet or sweat it off? You get someone to cut off all your hair.

It worked. Bald Vinci lost the 200 grams and won the gold medal.

Mechanic!!!

One of the most highly anticipated races at the 1992 Olympics was the wheelchair sprint. It was only a demonstration event, but it was the first test for people who wanted to see wheelchair events included in the Games.

Millions tuned in on TV.

Canada's Jeff Adams was tops in the world and had waited for this moment for years. He looked like he had a lock on victory — until one of his wheels fell off. Adams slammed his chair in frustration as other racers passed him.

Adams vowed he'd be back. And he was. He competed at the 1996, 2000 and 2004 Games. And won multiple medals at the Paralympic Games. In 2004, in Athens, he even climbed the Acropolis in his wheelchair.

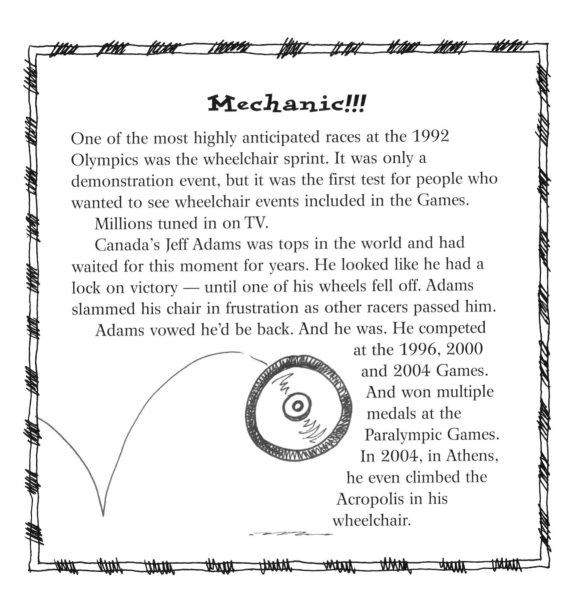

Anybody got a match?

One of the most honored traditions of the Games is the Olympic Flame. It's first lit by the rays of the sun in a big ancient-Greek-type ceremony featuring dancing women and wheat. That flame is then taken to wherever the next Games are to be held and used to light the cauldron that burns throughout the Games.

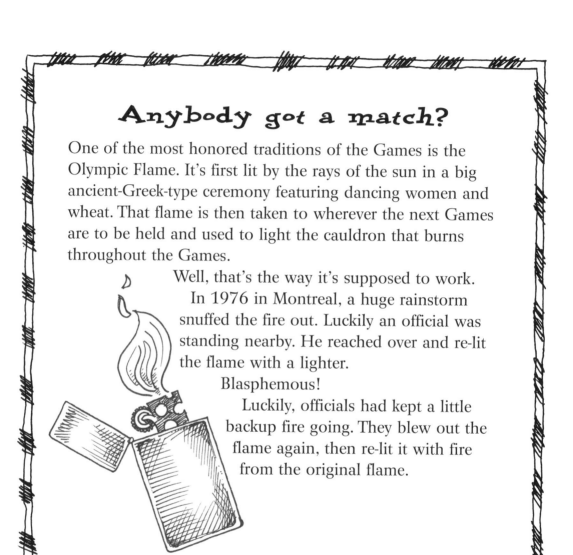

Well, that's the way it's supposed to work.

In 1976 in Montreal, a huge rainstorm snuffed the fire out. Luckily an official was standing nearby. He reached over and re-lit the flame with a lighter.

Blasphemous!

Luckily, officials had kept a little backup fire going. They blew out the flame again, then re-lit it with fire from the original flame.

First photo finish

During the first few Games, officials used their naked eyes to judge who finished in the medals, but that changed in 1932.

U.S. athlete Jack Keller was awarded the bronze medal in the 110-meter hurdles. Afterward (a bit too late), officials decided to look at photos of the finish line, because it was such a close race.

Oops — Britain's Donald Finlay had actually beat Keller by a nose (or a leg). A real classy guy, Keller sought out Finlay at the athletes' village and personally handed over the bronze.

JUMP SOME REAL HURDLES

Every athlete has to overcome something: a bad cold, a hurt toe, a broken alarm clock — whatever.

Some have to overcome way more than that.

This chapter is about people who refused to let anything stop them.

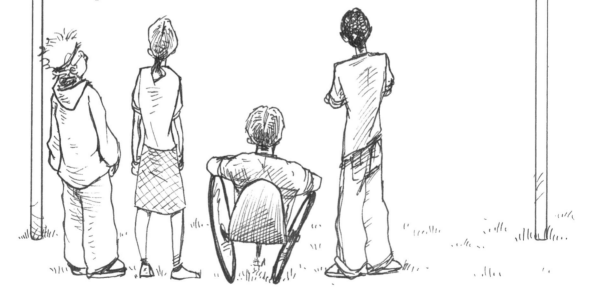

Rockheads

Hassiba Boulmerka was one of the most successful runners of all time. When she won the 1500-meter race at the 1991 World Championships, she became a national hero, but not everyone back home in Algeria was happy about her success.

Some people opposed her wearing clothes that showed her bare legs and arms. Fanatics would line her practice route and hurl insults and, sometimes, stones. When Boulmerka criticized them publicly, the tension increased. She even received death threats.

She decided to move to Italy, where she could train without being harassed. Good decision. The next year she won gold in the Olympic 1500-meter race in Barcelona.

A fool for school

Haile Gebrselassie grew up poor on a farm in Ethiopia, where he had lots of chores. But he still wanted to go to school, even though it was ten kilometers away. So Gebrselassie ran. He ran ten kilometers to school each morning, after chores, and ten kilometers back each afternoon, for more chores.

All that running paid off. Gebrselassie became one of the best distance runners ever. He won Olympic gold in the 10 000-meter race twice — in 1996 and 2000. You could recognize him by the slight crook in his arm, a habit he formed while carrying those schoolbooks.

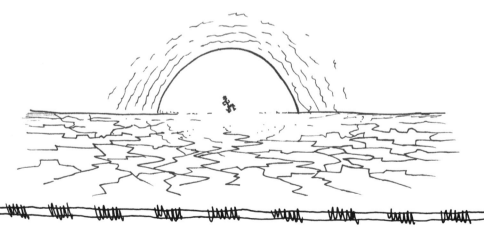

Thugs couldn't stop Thugwane

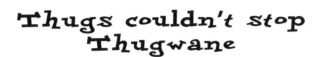

A gunshot traditionally starts every race.

A gunshot almost ended Josia Thugwane's career.

Thugwane made history in the 1996 marathon: he was the first black South African to win an Olympic gold medal, but he almost didn't make it to the race. Just weeks before the Olympics, thieves opened fire on his car. A bullet grazed Thugwane's chin, but he wasn't too injured to compete.

Things got even worse after he won his gold medal. People saw his face on TV and figured that if he was famous he must also be rich. During a training run, three men beat him up. He lost some teeth and spent a week in hospital.

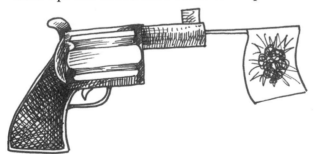

But he kept competing — so successfully that eventually he won enough money to buy a house with a security system.

After this, boxing is easy

Boxer Victor Ramos was pleased to represent East Timor at the Sydney Olympics in 2000, but he was happier just to be alive.

During East Timor's bloody civil war, militiamen attacked his home, spraying bullets everywhere. Ramos was hit in the stomach. (The scar is still there.)

This was a common story for many East Timorese, not just the athletes. Some hid in the jungle for weeks. By the time United Nations troops restored order, Ramos and

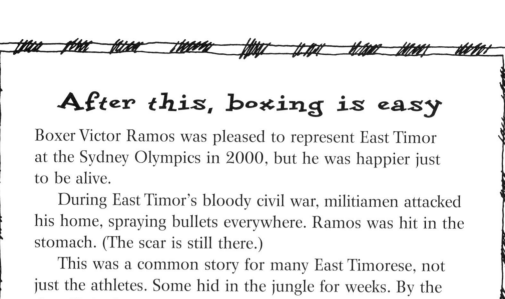

others returned home only to find that the militiamen had burned everything, including all their training equipment.

Olympic organizers stepped in to help. They paid for the athletes to move to Australia for the final few months before the Games to continue their training.

Medical miracle

If you'd met Wilma Rudolph when she was a little girl in Tennessee, you would have predicted a future with crutches, not Olympic medals.

Rudolph was born prematurely and suffered illness after illness. As a toddler, she was diagnosed with polio. Her family was told she'd never walk, but her mother scraped together all she could to get Wilma therapy. First Wilma learned to walk with a brace, then all on her own. Once the brace was off, Rudolph became obsessed with athletics.

She more than made up for lost time — at the 1960 Olympics in Rome, Rudolph won three gold medals in track and field.

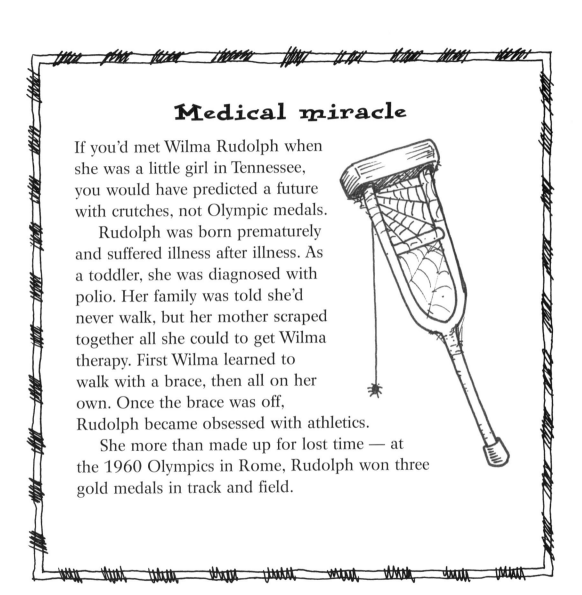

This guy had a legup on the competition...

American George Eyser was one of the most incredible Olympic champions. In 1904, he won three gold medals, two silvers and a bronze. The gold medals came in the demanding gymnastics events: the vault, parallel bars and

rope climbing. He also competed in the track-and-field events.

Here's something even more amazing — Eyser did all that with a wooden leg. His left leg had been removed after he'd been run over by a train.

EVENT #16
BLAST OFF INTO THE FUTURE

Lots of sports want to be included in the Olympics and, from time to time, new sports are added. Others are dropped. Things change.

Baseball and softball were in for a few years, but have been kicked out. Snowboarding and beach volleyball are currently in, as they appeal to younger fans.

So what sports might the kids be cheering for in the future? Here are some hopefuls the International Olympic Committee has put on the list for consideration.

Wushu

This is kind of like watching a martial arts movie and ballet at the same time.

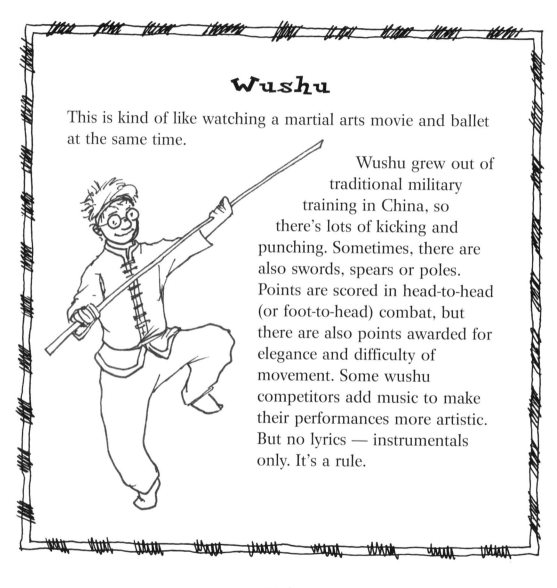

Wushu grew out of traditional military training in China, so there's lots of kicking and punching. Sometimes, there are also swords, spears or poles. Points are scored in head-to-head (or foot-to-head) combat, but there are also points awarded for elegance and difficulty of movement. Some wushu competitors add music to make their performances more artistic. But no lyrics — instrumentals only. It's a rule.

Korfball

"Korf" is the Dutch word for basket, and, yes, there's a ball, a basket and you score by shooting the ball into the basket. But it's not quite basketball.

Dutch schoolteacher Nico Broekhuysen invented the sport more than a hundred years ago, so both men and women could play. There are eight players per team, half of them male, half female. Passing is important, because you can't shoot if there's a defender between you and the basket.

Korfball has been growing in recent years as more men and women look to compete together. And it's also the one sport where being called a "Korfer" is a good thing.

Bridge

Right, the card game. It's a recognized sport.

That means it has to follow the Olympic rules, including anti-doping regulations.

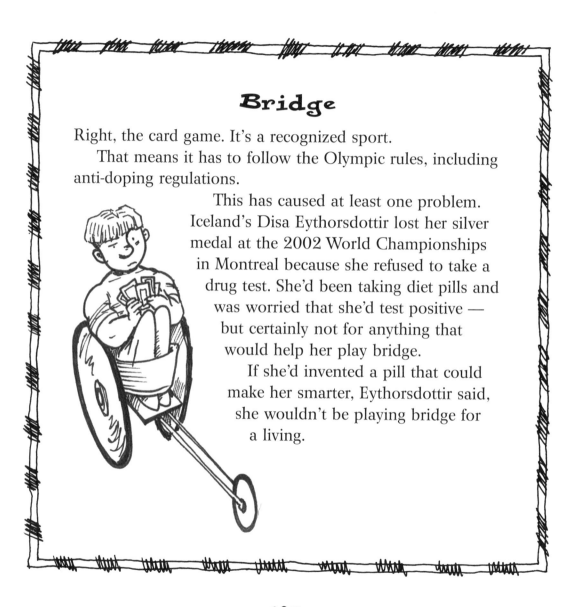

This has caused at least one problem. Iceland's Disa Eythorsdottir lost her silver medal at the 2002 World Championships in Montreal because she refused to take a drug test. She'd been taking diet pills and was worried that she'd test positive — but certainly not for anything that would help her play bridge.

If she'd invented a pill that could make her smarter, Eythorsdottir said, she wouldn't be playing bridge for a living.

Bandy

Bandy is kind of a cross between field and ice hockey. It's played on skates, but players hit a ball into the goal using field hockey sticks. It's also a bit like soccer, as the rink is the size of a soccer field and there are eleven players a side. Got all that?

Bandy is unlikely to make it to the Olympics, however. It costs a lot of money to build a rink the size of two hockey rinks, and the game is played almost exclusively in Northern Europe.

Air sports

This category includes everything from planes to balloons and hang gliders. But don't worry if you don't have a pilot's license or are afraid of heights. There are also competitions for model airplanes and model rockets.

Finally, a sport for all ages.

Dancesport

This one gets a lot of flak. The athletes wear dresses and tuxedos. They are judged on their rumbas, jives and waltzes. Even their foxtrots and cha-cha-chas.

Okay, so it's ballroom dancing, and critics say that's not a sport. Maybe, maybe not — but then, take a look at those figure-skating and synchro-swimming competitions.

And then there's ...

Pelote Basque

Powerboating

Billiards

Bowling

Netball

Sumo wrestling

Orienteering

Water skiing

Polo

HONEST!

THE FINISH LINE

And there you have it.

But Olympic Games happen every two years, so who knows what goofy stuff we'll have to talk about in the future.

See you there!

ANOTHER WACKY SPORTS COMPENDIUM BY KEVIN SYLVESTER!

Take a walk on the weird side!

Odd, weird and just plain gross moments in sports await you inside *Sports Hall of Weird*. With categories like Good Gusy Finish Last, Fans from Beyond the Grave, and Great Swindles and Cheats, you know you're in for a great time! From yucky bathroom accidents to cursed teams and spectacular losers, this hall's got it all.

ISBN 978-1-55337-635-4